Marcel Breuer

Arnt Cobbers

MARCEL BREUER

TASCHEN

HONG KONG KÖLN LONDON LOS ANGELES MADRID PARIS TOKYO

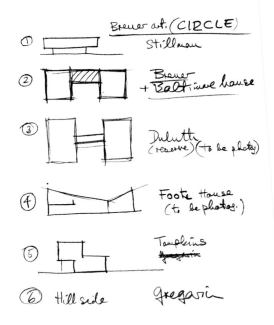

Illustration page 2 ▶ Marcel Breuer at the Whitney
Museum of American Art, 1967
Illustration page 4 ▶ Breuer's sketches of the
floorplans and elevation of the houses he
designed in America

©2007 TASCHEN GmbH
Hohenzollernring 53, D-50672 Köln
www.taschen.com

Editor ▶ Peter Gössel, Bremen
Conception and layout ▶ Gössel und Partner,
Bremen
Project management ▶ Eike Meyer, Bremen
Text edited by ▶ Avinus, Berlin
Translation ▶ Maureen Roycroft Sommer,
Bergisch Gladbach

Printed in Germany
ISBN-10: 978-3-8228-4887-6

Contents

Introducion

As early as 1956, *Time* magazine described Marcel Breuer as one of "The 20th Century Form Givers". At the age of only twenty-three, he made design history by creating tubular steel furniture. His "cantilever chair" became an icon of modern interior design. However, as an architect—and that is how Breuer saw himself—he belonged to a generation that has not fared well in retrospect. Nineteen years younger than Walter Gropius, sixteen years younger than Mies van der Rohe, and fifteen years younger than Le Corbusier, he arrived on the scene too late to play an active role in launching a new architectural age.

Breuer's finest hour as an architect came after the Second World War, when he designed a number of impressive buildings and found model solutions that were emulated by architects all over the world. To his misfortune, however, post-war Modernism has generally fallen into disregard—never really recovering from the criticism of postmodernists. Breuer's private homes, many of them in the Northeastern United States, are "timelessly" beautiful and functional, but ultimately lack revolutionary panache. After the mid-1950s, his major building projects tended to espouse a material that was soon ostracized by arbiters of contemporary taste: exposed concrete. To make matters "even worse", Breuer later cultivated façades made of prefabricated concrete elements. Such architecture today no longer serves as a model.

Yet Breuer was not only one of the most productive and commercially successful architects of the twentieth century, he was also one of the most innovative and interesting. He had a masterful sense of proportion, form and material. And anyone willing to approach his concrete architecture with an open mind, will discover an energy and qualities that are hard to resist.

Marcel Lajos Breuer was born on May 21, 1902 in the Hungarian town of Pécs, as the third and youngest child of the dentist Jakob Breuer and his wife Franciska. Little is known of his childhood, but art seems to have played an important role in his parents' home. After completing school, Breuer was awarded a scholarship to the Academy of Fine Arts in Vienna, but the few weeks he spent there he later called the unhappiest in his life. When he heard about a new art academy in Weimar, Breuer acted immediately. Soon the eighteen-year-old was among the 143 students who began their studies in the second year of the "Bauhaus"—thereby becoming part of a self-designated spearhead of the avant-garde.

After the mandatory Basic Course under Johannes Itten, Breuer trained as a cabinetmaker. He was apparently a gifted painter, since Oskar Schlemmer noted with regret, in his 1922 diary, that Breuer had given up painting altogether to concentrate on making furniture. He attracted quite a bit of attention in 1922 with his "Constructivist" slat chair, which became a much-discussed example of a new orientation at the Bauhaus—away from crafts and towards a "new unity of art and technology".

From 1923, Breuer pursued his interest in architecture, but never completed formal architectural training—there was none at the Bauhaus. Instead, he gained experience in Gropius's private office. In 1924–1925, he spent a couple of months in Paris where Le Corbusier apparently offered to hire him. Breuer, however, chose to direct the furniture workshop at the Bauhaus as one of the "young masters".

The three years in Dessau, the city to which the Bauhaus relocated in the spring of 1925, marked his breakthrough as a designer. Breuer designed the world's first tubular steel furniture, the club chair, which was later called "Wassily", along with other seating that played a role in determining the image of the Bauhaus. Yet Breuer wanted to become an architect—and felt limited in his personal development. Gropius always supported Breuer in whatever way he could, and a very close relationship soon developed between the two of them, which also included Gropius's wife Ise.

Breuer (like Gropius) left Dessau in January 1928 and moved to Berlin. Two doors down from where Gropius lived and worked, he opened his own architectural office. The timing could hardly have been worse. Building activity had come to a standstill because of the economic crisis, so Breuer spent most of his time working on entries for major competitions, including a 1,100-bed hospital in (Wuppertal-)Elberfeld and a theatre with seating for 4,000 in the Ukranian city of Kharkov.

Breuer, who had married the Bauhaus student Martha Erps in 1926, earned his living by marketing his metal furniture and doing interior design work for wealthy art-lovers. When these commissions also ceased, Breuer set off on a driving tour of Southern Europe and Morocco for several months. In a letter to Ise Gropius dated March 1932, he asked: "Should I spend the next nine years drawing up building plans without ever executing them? In that case, painting makes more sense. If only art wasn't so boring!"

The Slatted Chair ti 1a, 1922

Salvation in the form of a letter reached him while he was travelling; the industrialist Paul Harnischmacher commissioned him to build a house in Wiesbaden. And even in this very first project, Breuer achieved an architectural vernacular of his own. An important characteristic of Breuer's work is the additive principle, which is like playing with building blocks. He combined building elements dedicated to specific functions, often simple rectangular parts, in different ways by pushing them together, placing them next to each other, or even on top of each other. He also varied the heights of the ceilings and the angles of the roofs, but almost never—in contrast to Gropius, Mies or Le Corbusier—fused two building elements into one, or designed interlocking cubes. At most, he cut small terraces or recessed balconies into a building's volume.

This reflects a second characteristic of Breuer's buildings: they are closed units with clearly defined outer shells that are initially stretched smoothly and then given volume and mass. As early as 1926, he described the design of his *Kleinmetallhaus* (small metal house) by explaining that it had "neither columns, poles nor thick walls. The supporting structure consists of lines—the closer they come to expressing their structural symbol, the straight line, the better. The insulating, light-weight sheets are no longer walls—the closer they come to expressing their practical symbol, the perfectly flat plane, the better. The monumentality of sheer mass ... will be overshadowed by the daring of the most vibrant force, the monumentality of the spirit. Instead of the pyramids: the Eiffel Tower ..."

During the 1950s Breuer became more and more fascinated by the "monumentality of mass" and, interestingly, he later developed a fancy for Egyptian architecture. Despite this aesthetic transformation, Breuer still adhered to the ideal of the supporting outer shell. He seldom designed curtain-wall façades—one of the most important

Farkas Molnár's flat in Budapest, 1929
Breuer's B9 tea table in three sizes and his B5
chair next to a painting by Sándor Bortnyik

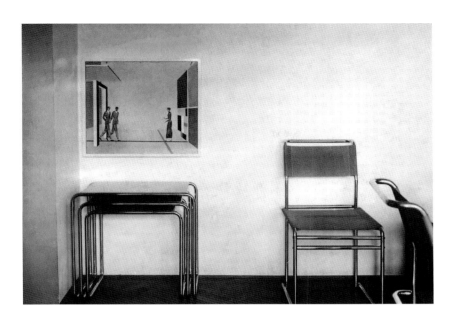

Kleinmetallhaus (small metal house) study,
1926

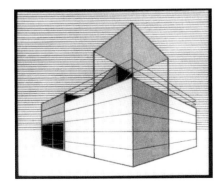

innovations in modern architecture—because he found supports in the middle of rooms enormously disturbing. He preferred to conceal supports in external and internal walls, even if this limited his freedom to design façades. He even preferred dividing large glass surfaces into frames, rather than installing architectural supports in front of, or behind, glass walls.

The Harnischmacher House was featured in many publications and became quite well known, but never led to subsequent commissions, and Breuer left Germany in late 1933. His Jewish background was apparently never an issue; even his long-term partners thought—up until the big 1981 Breuer exhibition in New York—that he was Catholic. After all, he had built a number of monasteries and churches in the 1950s and 1960s.

For two years he was involved in an unsuccessful architectural firm with Farkas Molnár and Jozsef Fischer in Budapest. At that time he also worked on the Doldertal Houses (multi-family dwellings) in Zurich. Again, Walter Gropius, who had been living in London since 1934, came to his aid by introducing him to a twenty-eight-year-old architect with building experience. This enabled Breuer, who had yet to speak a word of English, to establish a joint practice with Francis Reginald Stevens Yorke in November 1925, thereby qualifying for a visa to remain in Great Britain.

During the next two years he designed some furniture—in plywood—as well as interiors, a few residential buildings and two important contributions to exhibitions: a model for the "Garden City of the Future", sponsored by the British Cement and Concrete Association, which was his first opportunity to work with concrete; and a pavilion for the Gane Furniture Company at the 1936 Bristol Agricultural Show, marking Breuer's first use of fieldstone masonry.

The fact he did not view this as a repudiation of Modernism, is reflected in a letter in which he wrote: "The use of traditional and new materials, and the transformation of traditional ideas into contemporary ones, leads to the creation of new forms and should not be equated with regression, but rather with innovation within the modern

movement." The early modernist dogma of "material honesty" seems to have been of little interest to Breuer later when he faced wooden and brick walls with fieldstone.

Gropius had, in the meantime, become a professor at Harvard University and paved the way for Breuer to follow him in 1937. "I'm going to become a Harvard professor, Gropius organized the whole thing," he wrote to a friend. "It's not such a demanding job, three afternoons a week, and still very prestigious and relatively well-paid. ... I'm happy I came to America, it's a great country."

With Gropius as the head of the department and Breuer as an associate professor of architecture, the Graduate School of Design became a Mecca for students with avant-garde leanings, including Edward Larrabee Barnes, John Johansen, Philip Johnson, Ieoh Ming Pei, Paul Rudolph and Harry Seidler. Breuer was a popular teacher, who called for unorthodox and innovative proposals on the part of his students. He showed them how to solve formal and functional problems without expecting them to espouse any particular style.

They were often invited to his recently built house in Lincoln, outside of the city, where he settled with his second wife Connie in 1940. She had been a secretary in the architectural office maintained by Gropius and Breuer ("Connie was a pretty good secretary but I thought she'd make an even better wife."). Throughout his life, Breuer valued interaction with young people. He was a figure of authority, who later never really let go of the reins in his office, but also a team worker who made people feel comfortable and had co-workers call him Lajkó (as did his friends)—a familiar form of his middle name. His friend Ieoh Ming Pei characterized Breuer as a simple, "down to

Marcel Breuer and Francis Redinald Stevens Yorke, Sea Lane House, Angmering-on-Sea, Sussex, England, 1936–1937, view from the southwest

The living room and dining room are located on the upper level behind the curving terrace. The side wing features six bedrooms in a row along the same hallway.

Garden City of the Future, London, England, 1936
Photograph of a model

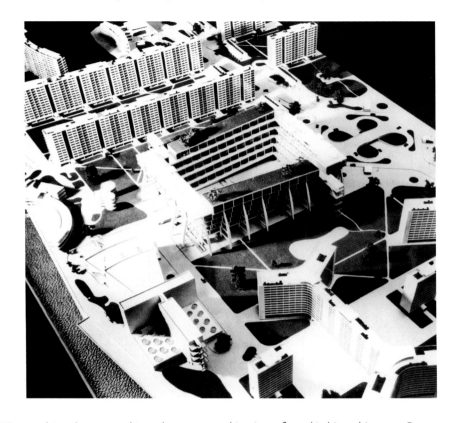

Ventris apartment in London, 1936
With a cabinet for the radio and record player in the living room

earth" and yet very cultivated man—a combination reflected in his architecture. Breuer was somewhat reserved, but friendly. He told great stories (particularly about his Bauhaus days), had a passion for cooking goulash and was a real film buff. At the same time he had an iron will and "liked the idea of being the best", as one of his associates put it. The only thing printed on his visiting card was "Marcel Breuer". He expected everyone to know the name.

Along with holding chairs as university professors, Breuer and Gropius also maintained a joint architectural office in Cambridge. Most of the demand was for detached houses, which were of little interest to Gropius, so he often left the work to Breuer, who was still happy to take on every commission. However, they still signed jointly on all of the projects.

Over the course of time, Breuer must have sensed a need to step out of this father figure's shadow. Hence, they split up in May 1941. A trifling matter triggered it—Gropius arrived late for a jury meeting, Breuer complained, and Gropius answered too brusquely. Breuer announced his resignation from their joint practice and began to work independently. After a period of hurt feelings, their friendship seems to have continued until Gropius died in 1969.

Although Gropius had opened many doors for Breuer over the years, he needed no help in establishing himself among New York's foremost architects—thanks to his concept for a "bi-nuclear house". Based on the idea of organizing living spaces according to functions; with "dynamic" daytime activities located in one part of the house, and quiet, private and contemplative phases of daily—or nightly—life located in an-

other. The Geller House, built near New York in 1944, was featured in the most important American lifestyle magazines. It fitted in perfectly with the spirit of the time.

After the war, the United States experienced a tremendous building boom. Anyone who could, hired a famous architect to design a custom-built house. Breuer was soon seen as the master of "informal living", the ideal of American interior design at that time: close to nature, uncomplicated, within a family circle. Marcel Breuer proved that Modernism and comfortable surroundings were not necessarily contradictions. His houses were suited for families with children, functional and still "stylish", sometimes even glamorous.

Breuer rarely designed floor plans with one room leading into another—he considered that impractical. As a rule, the living and dining room, and sometimes the kitchen, were located in a main room, divided only by a fireplace or furniture. In general, Breuer looked upon furniture as an essential element in structuring space, i.e. as an integral part of architecture. He usually separated bedrooms and studies, in his "bi-nuclear houses" they were located in separate sections. The patterns of use, upon which his limited number of floor plan variations is based, are extremely schematic and simplified—yet many clients found the system convincing.

Breuer built nearly sixty homes, most of them by the mid-1950s. Each of them has an individual character—and yet all of them are oriented to two basic models: the "longhouse" (with a simple rectangular floor plan and, at best, a few smaller additions) and the "bi-nuclear house". In a very few cases, Breuer arranged the other sections around a two-storey centre, but most of his homes are single-storey buildings or erected on raised foundations.

Once a solution had proved viable, Breuer adhered to it tenaciously. His avowed goal was to develop a typology, a repertoire of model solutions. In a famous lecture entitled "Where do we stand today?", held at the Kunstgewerbemuseum in Zurich in

Tompkins House, Hewlett Harbor, Long Island, New York, 1945–1946
Staggering the two floors created a large sun terrace facing south, and a covered parking space facing the street.

1934, he said, "We are searching for what is typical, the norm, the obvious form, the deliberate solution ... fantasy does not express itself today in abstract adventures of the spirit, but rather in the ability to bring the fantastic world of reality into a characteristic order."

At the same time Breuer always emphasized the need to re-examine existing standards in order to keep them from becoming paralyzed in sterility. He considered experimentation to be "one of the responsibilities of an architect". Thus, Breuer not only discovered revolutionary new applications for tubular steel, as a young master at the Bauhaus, but also for the balloon frame (the self-supporting walls used in traditional wooden houses in America), in the 1940s, and later for concrete. When the spectacular cantilever balcony on his first house in New Canaan—which was only supported by steel cables—began to collapse in 1947, Breuer simply told his employees: "That's what you call an experiment."

The Breuer family, now including son Tamas (called Tom), moved into a new house without sensational structural innovations four years later—a bungalow that was also located in the wealthy suburb of New Canaan. Breuer's New York office was doing so well that he never returned to Harvard after taking a sabbatical in 1946. The model house erected in the garden of the Museum of Modern Art (MoMA) in New York in 1949 made him even more popular, and eventually larger commissions followed: for a library and a college dormitory, for schools, office buildings and commercial properties.

A turning point came in 1952. With considerable lobbying on the part of Walter Gropius, who was the chairman of the advisory committee, Breuer was selected as one of three architects to design the UNESCO headquarters in Paris. This had important consequences: Breuer developed a second base of operations in Europe, and he received a growing number of major commissions. By the end of the 1950s Breuer had

become one of the first jetsetters in the architectural world, always travelling between his offices in New York, Paris and, for a while, also Caracas. He was also consulted about a number of building projects in Asia, which were ultimately never built.

The cooperation in Paris with Pier Luigi Nervi, the structural engineer so famous for his concrete buildings, again brought Breuer into contact with the material that was to become characteristic of his work in the following years. "I believe the architect can fully express himself as an artist by means of concrete," he said in 1973. He was the first architect from the United States for whom concrete played a major role, and it allowed him the freedom to create wide overhangs, sloping roofs and walls that were folded or rotated on their own axes.

He was fascinated by hyperbolic paraboloids, a surface that rotates within itself, a form used in Latin American architecture. Breuer's cast concrete works possess great sculptural power and plasticity, especially his churches—and their bell towers. Breuer paid great attention to detail, including the texture of his materials: the impression left by the form boards, as well as the colour, coarseness and the pattern of the exposed concrete, the shape of the stones used in natural stone walls, the orientation of wooden slats. For each of his later major projects, he sought new variations in the stark relief of the prefabricated concrete elements that created a vibrant interplay of light and

Robinson House, Williamstown,
Massachusetts, 1946–1948

Alworth/Starkey House, Duluth, Minnesota, 1954–1955
Breuer loved to play around with sloping sites. From the living areas, the house has a magnificent view of Lake Superior.

shadow. Marcel Breuer had a masterful understanding of how to combine different materials—a legacy of his years at the Bauhaus, where the consideration of the aesthetic and functional qualities of different materials played a central role. The "principle of contrast" was essential to him. He not only contrasted materials, in the 1940s he also started using bright red and blue surfaces as colour accents in his buildings, in which natural tones or black, white and grey otherwise predominated.

In his Harnischmacher House the black and white striped awning, which mitigated the severity of its clean lines, caused a stir. Here, again, it is typical that a functional detail played an aesthetic role. Hence, there are certain elements that are recurrent in Breuer's work: the open fireplace as the "heart" of the house, and each of them a unique design; the open, exterior stairways; the massive, often white, cornices projecting out from underneath the roofs, the canopies over the entrances; and the ubiquitous solar protection elements. He often used trapezoidal forms in floor plans and in elevations, as well as elongated rectangles, and large surfaces broken up by stripes or other geometric patterns. He avoided "L" and "S" forms whenever he could.

In 1956, Breuer was able to secure the loyal, long-term cooperation of three architects, all twenty-five years his junior, Herbert Beckhard, Hamilton Smith and Robert F. Gatje (and later also Tician Papachristou); he made them "associates" in his practice with the option of becoming equal partners after ten years, without requiring any capital investment. Yet Breuer continued to determine what went on in the office, which had roughly thirty employees in the 1960s. "No designs ever leave my office until I have worked out, or at least supervised, every detail." As a rule, Breuer sketched the initial design and one of the partners worked it out.

Breuer was, like Gropius, not a good draughtsman, and quipped that "I could never have gotten a job in this office". He was proud of the fact that many of his projects remained below the estimated budget. In his opinion, the aspect of cost was another argument in favour of concrete. This was especially true of the façades made of pre-fabricated modules, a system that he developed in 1960 for the IBM research centre in La Gaude, France, and often used thereafter—including at the ski resort Flaine in the French Alps and for a satellite city for 15,000 inhabitants built near Bayonne.

The Whitney Museum, which was Breuer's only building in Manhattan, was completed in 1966, and was a great success. His reputation did, however, become somewhat tarnished after he proposed a fifty-five-storey office tower over Grand Central Station, a project that historic preservationists were able to block. Breuer was still awarded honorary doctorates and professorships, and celebrated in exhibitions. His office even weathered the building crisis of the early 1970s relatively well. Neither the criticism lodged against Modernism, nor the innovations formulated by postmodernists captured his interest.

From the mid-1960s on Marcel Breuer had been plagued by problems with his heart and had had trouble sleeping. In 1973 a massive heart attack forced him to slow down. On March 1, 1976 he finally had to announce his resignation from active employment. "It's like losing my right arm!" he wrote to a friend. His partners continued to operate under the name "Marcel Breuer Associates" for several years. Breuer died in New York on July 1, 1981. Three weeks later, the MoMA opened a major solo exhibition

Armstrong Rubber Company, West Haven, Connecticut, 1967–1970
The offices of the company headquarters "float" on four levels over the research and development department.

University of Massachusetts, Murray Lincoln Campus Center, Amherst, Massachusetts, 1965–1970
The façade reflects the different uses of each level (from bottom to top): dormitory, offices and restaurants. There is additional space for shops and a cafeteria below ground at foundation level.

on Breuer focussing on design and interior decorating. By that point in time, his architecture was no longer really appreciated. It is, however, high time that its qualities were rediscovered.

1923 – 1925 · Furniture from the Woodworking Shop

Display Case, 1925

"A chair, for example," wrote Marcel Breuer in 1923, "should not be horizontal-vertical, also not Expressionistic, Constructivist, conceived solely for functionality, and also not designed to 'match' a table, it should just be a good chair, and then it will match a good table." It is this approach, free of all dogmatism and theory, that allowed Breuer to come up with fundamentally new solutions time and again, both as a designer and an architect. And, yet, it is surprising how quickly he found his own language of form.

The first piece of furniture designed and built by Breuer was his Expressionistic "African chair" of 1921, which has only been preserved as a photograph. It is an impressive, hand-carved and hand-painted throne-like piece with a seat and backrest made of stiffly woven textiles from the weaver's workshop. That same year Breuer completed two massive chairs and a table that was no less substantial for the entrance hall to Gropius's House Sommerfeld in Berlin. The "Constructivist", slatted chair (ti 1a; ti as a short form of the German word for woodworking shop) influenced by De Stijl furniture was created in 1922, and this basic orientation was to play a determining role in Breuer's future work. Working as a journeyman (as of late 1923) and as the director (as of 1925) of the furniture workshop, Breuer designed collections of furniture for children and the kitchen, which were produced in series—quite a success as far as Bauhaus products are concerned—as well as other furniture. His first architectural designs exhibit the same language of form. Hence, the 1924 model for a stacked high-rise is strongly reminiscent of a shelf unit that Breuer designed that same year. The form of the first tubular steel chairs is clearly reflected in Breuer's wooden chairs. The shift to the new material represented a small—yet ingenious—step.

Chair for the House Sommerfeld, 1921
Cherry wood, red and black leather

Opposite page:
Vitrine ti 66b, 1926

1925–1932 · Tubular Steel Furniture

Recliner in the Gropius House in Dessau, 1925

Purportedly, the handlebars of a bicycle inspired the twenty-three-year-old Marcel Breuer in discovering what was ultimately to be an extraordinary stroke of genius. Breuer, who had recently been named director of the furniture workshop, had tubular steel sent to him in Dessau—the bicycle manufacturer Adler found the matter absurd, but Mannesmann reacted promptly—and he used it to create the world's first tubular steel chair with the help of a mechanic from the Junker aircraft company.

Breuer's highly acclaimed 1922 slat chair was influenced by De Stijl furniture and his original version of the tubular steel chair, preserved only as a photograph, seems like an adaptation of Gerrit Rietveld's 1917 "red/blue chair" in a new material. "Looking at my first tubular steel club chair when it was completed, I thought that this is the one piece of work for which I will be criticized most. Its outward appearance and material expression are most extreme; it is the least artistic, the most logical, the least 'hospitable', the most machine-like. And just the opposite happened," Breuer said in 1927.

Breuer re-worked the design of the chair, which originally stood on four legs and displayed obvious signs of welding, three times before finding the ultimate form in 1927. This "final version" with runners, a closed backrest, and joints that only need to be screwed together, as well as belts and seats made of "Eisengarn", has been marketed since 1962 under the name "Wassily". After Breuer and a fellow Hungarian called Kálmán Lengyel established Standard-Möbel in Berlin to produce and market the furniture in 1926–1927, the chair was given the catalogue number B3 (B for Breuer).

Gropius was so taken with Breuer's designs that he assigned him the task of furnishing most of the new school building. Breuer developed a stool (B9) for the cafeteria, which was produced in four sizes and could also be used as a side table. It soon became very popular. He designed a series of folding chairs for the assembly hall as well as studio tables and chairs, and a folding armchair. His "metal furniture" (Breuer's term) contributed decisively to the Bauhaus image—in Dessau, at major exhibitions and in publications. Plated with nickel or chrome, tubular steel furniture, which was soon designed by others as well, became a classic manifestation of "New Living"—objective, functional, convenient, lightweight, hygienic and practical.

The first Standard-Möbel catalogue, issued in 1927, described the collection, which comprised only ten products, in the following way: "A model has been developed for every requirement and improved to the point where no variation is possible." When Gropius heard about Breuer's company, there was quite a disagreement. Breuer argued that other Bauhaus masters sold their paintings for their own profit, and Gropius finally accepted that the Bauhaus was not entitled to a share of the commercial success. It was, however, modest—Standard-Möbel produced small series in a little workshop—so Breuer signed his rights over to the company in 1928 for a share of the profits. That same year Breuer signed a contract with the well-known furniture company Thonet, for which he designed a variety of tubular steel furniture in the following years, including the cantilever chair B32. It was soon the centre of a controversy regarding the copyright to the design.

Left page:
Bauhaus Dessau, 1925
The auditorium with Breuer's B1 folding chairs

Model estate at Weissenhof, Stuttgart, 1927
Breuer furnished the interior of House 16,
designed by Gropius.

The Cantilever Chair B33, 1928

In 1927 the Dutch designer Mart Stam had presented a chair made of steel tubing bent at a ninety-degree angle, without back legs, but also without bounce. Stam had already sketched his idea in Stuttgart in 1926. Mies van der Rohe then took the idea and developed it into a more refined, cantilever chair with rounded legs and bounce, for which he received a patent in 1928.

Breuer's cantilever chair first appeared in the 1929 Standard-Möbel catalogue. It is similar to Stam's model, except that it swings thanks to the thicker tubing and the nickel plating. In addition, the backrest is bent back slightly at the lower edge of the webbing, making it much more comfortable to sit in. And only in this form, as designed by Breuer, did the chair become a worldwide and often copied success—both with and without armrests. Breuer later claimed that Stam had stolen the idea from him at the Bauhaus, a claim Stam always disputed.

A long legal battle ensued between Anton Lorenz, the last director and legal representative of Standard-Möbel, and Thonet, which produced different cantilever chair models according to the designs by Breuer and Stam. Finally, in 1932, the Leipzig High Court recognized Mart Stam (and Lorenz) as the holder(s) of the artistic copyright for

The Standard-Möbel catalogue offered the B9 stool as a "tea table" in four sizes.

the cubic chair without back legs. Breuer thereby lost an appreciable source of income from the licence fees as of 1933. Through a bizarre coincidence, Lorenz began working as a patent specialist for Thonet shortly thereafter and commissioned Stam to re-examine Breuer's models. Stam made sure that the characteristic "Breuer bend" was eradicated from those Thonet chairs no longer designated as Breuer's designs.

In 1962 Gavina, an Italian manufacturer, approached Breuer requesting his authorization and cooperation in bringing his classics back onto the market. The club chair B3 became the "Wassily" (Breuer's homage to Kandinsky) and the cantilever chair became the "Cesca" (after Breuer's daughter). Since 1968 they have been produced and marketed by the American company Knoll in great numbers. These two classics of modern furniture design are again in great demand by people who can afford stylish interior design. However, Breuer's furniture never did come to be used by a wide cross section of the population, as had been foreseen in the Bauhaus days—even then wooden furniture was much cheaper to produce. Ever since a court in Cologne made a final ruling in 1989, Thonet has been selling Breuer's cantilever chair in Germany with a note: "Design Marcel Breuer—artistic copyright Mart Stam".

The B3 "Club Chair", now known as "Wassily"

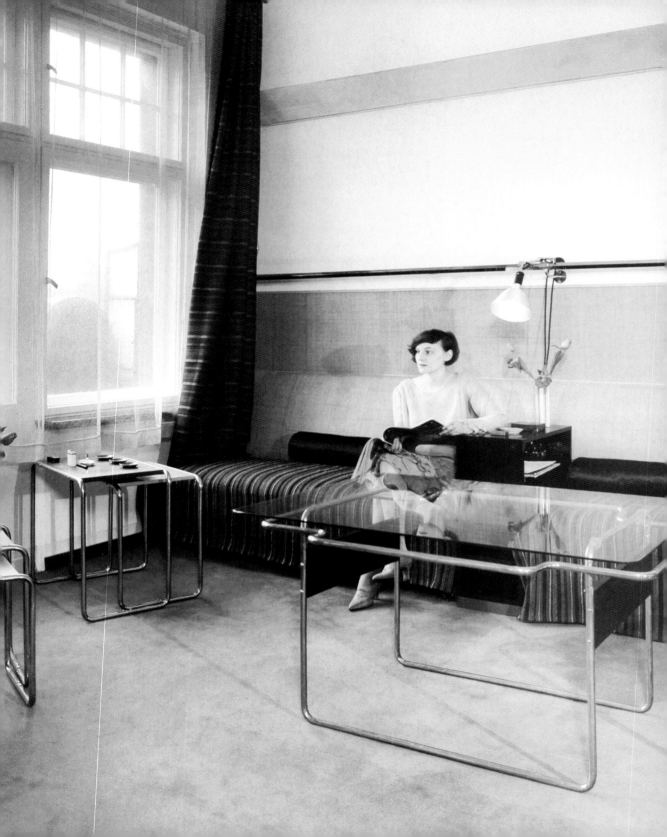

1927 ‣ Interior Design for Piscator
Berlin, Germany

The dining room with one of Breuer's typical sideboards

The master bedroom

While still at the Bauhaus, Breuer received several commissions to design interiors. The most important of these came from Berlin theatre director Erwin Piscator. Piscator's wife Hildegard gave Breuer the following instructions: "Don't take anything from the old flat ... Start with the very basics and create everything from the front door through to the pantry door in the same style. Only as much furniture as is necessary, so there is enough space."

Breuer took an appropriately radical approach to the five-room flat. He had new doors hung and the walls painted in light colours. He replaced freestanding wardrobes and cupboards with built-in furniture. Apart from that, he only used his model furniture. He compensated for the coolness of the steel tubing and glass tables with carpets, curtains and upholstery. He opened up the living room and dining room by creating a wide opening in the wall between them, where he installed a sliding door. Across the entire back wall of the dining room he had a shallow hanging cabinet installed, an element that was to become Breuer's trademark. Half of the Piscators' bedroom was designed as a gym—an indication of the health and body consciousness of the 1920s.

Featured in numerous magazines, the Piscators' flat became a model of modern interior design. Redesigning the interiors of homes and flats for wealthy patrons of the arts became Breuer's main occupation during his years in Berlin. All of his interiors are characterized by sparseness and sobriety, as well as a certain light-handed elegance. The famous art historian Julius Posener expressed his reservations about them by saying that "these rooms always have a severe influence on my deportment and I feel embarrassed when I don't think I can live up to their expectations."

1927▸Young Masters' Houses BAMBOS
Dessau, Germany ▸ not realized

Model of BAMBOS 1
Reconstruction based on a design by
Marcel Breuer

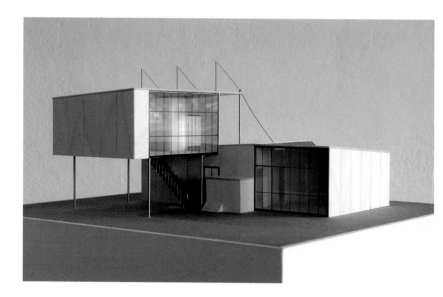

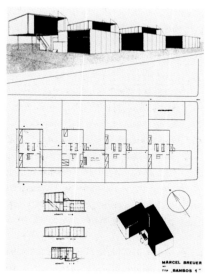

BAMBOS Type 1
Perspective drawing, floor plan, cross sections
and axonometric view
The first issue of the *Bauhauszeitschrift* (Bauhaus
magazine) in 1928

After the move to Dessau, seven studio houses were built for the Bauhaus masters along with the school buildings. The former students in charge of the workshops, the "young masters", felt disadvantaged living in the big studio building. It took until 1927 for Gropius to appropriate money for the construction of a "small group of houses", which were to be built across from the new school building according to Breuer's plans. Financial problems and resistance from the German Ministry of Labour delayed the project. When Breuer left the Bauhaus in January 1928, the idea of building the houses for the young masters was abandoned.

Breuer developed three types of modest "steel skeleton structures with dry-wall filling material". Their walls were to be made of prefabricated sheets of asbestos cement. Only one of the BAMBOS houses, as they were called in reference to their future residents Herbert Bayer, Josef Albers, Hannes Meyer, Marcel Breuer, Otto Meyer-Ottens and Joost Schmidt, was foreseen for construction in a row of six houses. All three types consisted of two building segments arranged differently. Type 1 combined two rectangular blocks. The larger residential segment measured 230 square feet and had two main rooms. The entrance, kitchen and bathroom were between these rooms. The second, smaller box rested partially on the roof of the first and on supports and was accessed via an external stairway, planned as a studio with a roof terrace.

Many of these elements—the adding together of two separate building segments, the strict separation between living and working spaces, building segments resting on supports, the slight angle of both roofs, steel cable used to suspend the overhanging roof of the studio, and the external stairway—were to become typical elements of Breuer's residential architecture.

26

1932 · Harnischmacher House
Wiesbaden, Germany

Garden view from the southeast in the winter (without awnings)

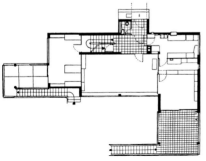

Floor plan of the main level and the study, located on an elevated level

Paul Harnischmacher, the general director of the Erdal shoe polish company, asked Breuer to build him a new house in the spring of 1932. Breuer had already designed the interior of Harnischmacher's office in Mainz and his flat in Wiesbaden. He was so excited about receiving his first building commission that he interrupted his tour of Southern Europe. By December of that year the house was ready for occupancy.

"Funds are limited—but building is cheap in Germany now," Breuer noted during the design phase. He then developed an amazingly mature first work based on functional necessities. The three-storey house was located on the far corner of a sloping property and had hardly any windows facing the street and the house next door. Most of the windows and terraces were oriented towards the south and west, providing views of the garden and the Rhine Valley. "The terraces and part of the block-like house are raised up on supports, forfeiting as little of the property as possible to the building space, the garden is still very large," Breuer explained. "In autumn, winter and spring, the sun helps with the heating. In summer, detachable cloth awnings provide protection from the sun."

Because it was on a slope, the main entrance led to the middle floor. This is where the living room and the dining room, which could be closed off by a sliding door, the kitchen and built-in china cabinet were located. Two bedrooms, a guestroom, a maid's room and a bathroom were on the upper floor. The dining room opened onto a cantilevered veranda, resting on supports, which provided access to the garden via a stairway. The roof over this veranda served as a terrace for the upper storey. A study was located in a separate section at the front of the house, over the garage and raised half a storey. It had a second veranda in front of it with another stairway leading to the

The living room

View from the living room

garden. The clearly defined living areas inside the house were mirrored on the outside. The individual building segments: main building, veranda and garage/office are put together like building blocks.

The building is a steel skeleton structure with supports integrated into the external and internal walls. Hence, Breuer did not have a free hand in designing the garden façade and had to interrupt the ribbon windows by including supports.

Contrasts between the white walls, the polished black of the wooden furniture and the silver sheen of the tubular steel are characteristic of the interior. Lighting was provided by spotlights installed on the walls and directed at the ceiling.

The Harnischmacher House was discussed in numerous architectural magazines and became relatively famous. However, it never led to subsequent commissions for Breuer, since Hitler became the chancellor of Germany only a month after it was

Marianne Harnischmacher in the living room

completed—and the blossoming of *Neues Bauen* (International Style) in Germany was precluded.

The house did not survive for very long, either—it was completely destroyed in the Second World War. Breuer built a new house for the Harnischmachers (a bungalow) on a neighbouring site in 1953–1954, which Paul Harnischmacher was so pleased with that he left Breuer a painting by Paul Klee in his will.

1933–1936 ▸ Doldertal Houses
Zurich, Switzerland ▸ with Emil and Alfred Roth

Opposite page:
View from the southeast

Drawing in perspective of the project's fourth draft when three buildings were still planned.

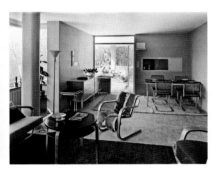

The living room of the model apartment, 1936
Featuring furniture by Marcel Breuer, Alvar Aalto and Alfred Roth

The multi-family dwellings in the Doldertal area of Zurich rank among the most famous buildings of the 1930s. Two steel skeleton structures, one diagonally behind the other, had walls of masonry between steel members and ceilings of cast concrete. The identical buildings had raised foundations set back behind concrete columns, providing space for garages, a laundry and storage. The first floor has a five-room and a one-room flat, the second floor has a six-room flat and there is a two-flat penthouse on the roof. All of the flats, with the exception of the one-room flat, have access to terraces that are cut into the otherwise cubic exterior of the building.

There was a long debate about the contributions made by each of the three architects involved in the project. The cousins Alfred and Emil Roth were apparently developing a tri-partite residential ensemble on a building site owned by Sigfried Giedion, an art historian and general secretary of the international architects' organization CIAM. In the summer of 1933, Giedion sent the plans to Breuer in Budapest requesting his opinion. Breuer and Giedion knew each other from the Bauhaus, and Breuer had also designed the interiors of the shops owned by Wohnbedarf, Giedion's home furnishing company in Zurich and Basel. Breuer considered the designs "very good in essential aspects", yet still suggested some changes in the layout of the flats. Consequently, Giedion suggested the Roths should work together with Breuer and they agreed immediately. The designs were re-worked a number of times, twice only for the sake of securing a permit from the city building commission. The buildings were finally erected in 1935–1936 after the fifth general plan had been changed for the third time. Breuer only sporadically visited the construction site, which was supervised by Alfred Roth, who had already overseen construction for Le Corbusier at the *Weissenhof Siedlung* in Stuttgart in 1927. He made the greatest contribution to the final form of the two multi-family dwellings. Breuer's greatest influence was structural; the supporting steel members were integrated into the walls, as in the Harnischmacher House.

1935–1936 · Isokon Furniture

Armchair made of aluminium, 1934

"Plywood ahoy!" wrote Breuer in a 1935 letter to Gropius about the material that would intrigue him as a furniture designer in the following years, even though he was actually far more interested in working with aluminium. After losing the court battle for the copyright on the cantilever chair made of steel tubing in 1932, Breuer soon began to consider aluminium a means of developing it further. Breuer had the ingenious idea, which helped to determine the form of Isokon furniture, patented in Switzerland in October 1933. It involved cutting wider bands of aluminium into two strips, beginning just behind the end of the runners. One of the strands was bent to form the foot and the backrest, the other strand to form the armrests or the supporting structure—numerous variations were possible. All kinds of chairs and recliners could be created using two parallel strips connected to each other by the seats and backrests. The furniture was produced by Embru, a Swiss company, but never sold very well.

When Breuer came to London in 1935, Gropius had already introduced him to Jack Pritchard, whose company, Isokon, produced modern plywood and laminated wooden furniture. Breuer designed five pieces of furniture for Isokon during his two years in London. The most famous piece was the recliner, a 1:1 adaptation of his 1933 aluminium recliner in formed plywood. Innovative in terms of its design, although not as commercially successful, was the furniture with sides made of cut-out pieces of plywood. Breuer continued to design further "cut-out furniture" for some of his homes in America up until about 1950.

In 1936 he redesigned the flat inhabited by Dorothea Ventris, a patroness of the arts. In doing so, he created one of his most beautiful interiors by combining the "warmth" of Isokon plywood furniture with the "coolness" of tubular steel furniture.

Isokon laminated wooden chair, 1936

Opposite page:
Detail of the "Isobar" in the Isokon Building in Hampstead, London, 1937

1936 ‣ Gane's Pavilion

Bristol, England ‣ with Francis Reginald Stevens Yorke

The living room with a sliding door open to the terrace

Floor plan

In a letter written in 1958, Breuer named two buildings he was particularly proud of: the UNESCO Building and Gane's Pavilion. The small exhibition building, constructed for the Royal Agricultural Show in Bristol in the summer of 1936, was indicative of what Breuer would later create. Already in the summer of 1935, during his first stay in England, Breuer had redecorated the private home of furniture manufacturer Crofton Gane near Bristol. Gane then hired him as an artistic consultant to his company, P. E. Gane. One of his responsibilities was designing their trade fair exhibits.

The four-room pavilion, built on a man-made mound of earth, fascinatingly combined fieldstone walls with large, segmented glass windows under a flat wooden roof with a dominant white cornice. By using "Cotswold stone" (a honey-coloured oolitic limestone), Breuer drew upon a local building material and refrained, for the first time, from creating the taut, smooth, white walls that had been so characteristic of most early Modern buildings. He may have been inspired by his partner Francis Reginald Stevens Yorke's weekend house, which was built of the same material. Alvar Aalto and Le Corbusier, whose Villa de Mandrot Breuer had seen on his trip through France, had already worked with exposed masonry.

In order to display the full range of the company's products, the pavilion was laid out as a living room, bedroom, study and children's bedroom, with neither kitchen nor bathroom. The view of the house when approaching the entrance and its layout are reminiscent of Mies van der Rohe's residential architecture. But closer examination

View from the southwest
The entrance is situated behind the wall to the left

clearly shows that Breuer sought neither to create a flow of open space inside, nor to integrate the interior and exterior spaces by placing walls in what seems to be an unrestricted manner. The roof of the pavilion covered a simple rectangle and is extended only slightly further over the entrance. One narrow side slanted in at an angle, the exterior wall of the living room swung in, and the space between the living room and children's bedroom was opened up as a terrace with a partially open roof. A pier, set slightly forward, served as a support for the roof. Two other walls extended out beyond the area spanned by the roof, providing the layout with a certain drama. Although its form could not be easily recognized, it was still a conventional block, and the walls made of masonry, glass and birch veneer plywood enclosed classically proportioned rooms. They only seemed to be so open because there were no doors and the floor-to-ceiling openings between the rooms were wider than conventional doorways. The building, which was torn down after only a short time, was featured in many publications, as well as in the exhibition on modern British architecture at the MoMA in New York in 1937.

1938–1939 ▸ Breuer House I

Lincoln, Massachusetts ▸ with Walter Gropius

Opposite page:

View into the living room
A mobile by Breuer's friend Alexander Calder is suspended from the ceiling.

Current view from the south
The veranda has been transformed into a fully glazed living area, to the right an annex has been added.

In November 1938, Helen Storrow, a wealthy lady from Boston, made Breuer a generous offer: she asked him to build a house for himself out in the countryside at her expense and on her land and to pay her ten per cent of the building costs as his annual rent for as long as he lived in the house. Breuer's "bachelor's house"—even though he married in 1940—was completed by the summer of 1939. It was located within view of two buildings by Gropius, which were built under the same agreement. One of them was Gropius's own home, which was a year older, and the other was the Ford House. These three "model homes" gave Gropius and Breuer an opportunity to illustrate their concept of architecture, and they did quite a bit of entertaining in their homes.

The Breuer House, now somewhat altered and enlarged, is organized in three clearly separate building segments: the core area, which is a living room with a trapezoid-shaped floor plan, and a high ceiling and a wall of windows facing south. It is flanked to the east by a two-storey building segment with a partially open interior and, to the west, by a veranda which is separated by a convex, natural stone wall with a fireplace set into it. The living room opens onto a sunken dining room flanked by the kitchen and the maid's room. Upstairs there is a bedroom next to which the bathroom and a second bedroom are located. The upper level can be separated by a sliding door and a curtain. As a result of the "three-dimensional flow of the rooms" (Marcel Breuer's student Ieoh Ming Pei), the small house seems to be incredibly spacious. It was furnished with Breuer's plywood furniture. In the living room the natural stone wall, the

Opposite page:

The Breuers in their living room: he is seated in his Isokon chair, she is on the stairway leading up to the bedrooms.

On the lower right there is a view of the dining room.

Left:

The veranda

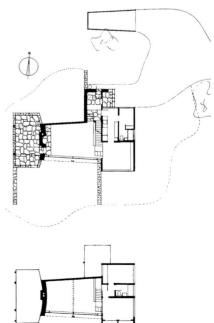

wide, segmented glass front and the wooden panelling on the back wall created exciting contrasts.

While the two-storey building section (with wooden walls made of vertically arranged slats) looks like a white cube from the outside, the living section and the veranda are highlighted by the prominent white cornice and twin wooden columns—motifs that were to take a firm place in Breuer's vernacular of forms.

1940–1941 ▸ Chamberlain Cottage
Wayland, Massachusetts ▸ with Walter Gropius

View from the west

Opposite page, above:
View from the back with the door to the garden

Opposite page, below:
The fireplace as a room divider and focal point of the house

Because they liked Marcel Breuer's house in Lincoln so much, the Chamberlains commissioned him to build them a weekend home in November 1940. It was completed in only four months. They expected Breuer to satisfy a number of clear demands on a limited budget: they wanted a house with a living room, dining room, bedroom, kitchen, bathroom and shelves for 1,000 books, as well as space for a workbench and a four-metre boat (for boating on a nearby river).

On a raised foundation of fieldstone, which was built into a slope and provided space for the boat and the workbench, Breuer set a flat-roofed wooden box measuring roughly 35 feet by 17 feet. One narrow side projects roughly 8 feet beyond the stone foundation. In front of the long north side a balcony seems to be suspended in air. On the long south side the entrance to the house is reached via a stairway built parallel to the exterior wall. A fireplace—the first in Breuer's oeuvre—divides the main room into a dining and a living area. This weekend house marked Breuer's final departure from "white Modernism".

The combination of a fieldstone foundation with a larger wooden box on top was to become characteristic of Breuer's architecture in the future. Breuer was only able to build the wide overhang and the extensive opening in the northern wall because of a special principle he used in its construction. It involved layering wood first horizontally (on the inside), then diagonally (in the middle) and finally vertically (outside) in order to ensure sufficient rigidity. Breuer described the process as creating "homemade plywood" or as "reinforced concrete made of wood". After it was seen in widely published photographs by Ezra Stoller, the little country house became an American icon of life in harmony with nature. Just as was the case with his own house, the Chamberlain Cottage was created in the office he shared with Gropius. It is, however, in terms of both its design and its execution, completely Breuer's work.

1944–1946 · Geller House I

Lawrence, Long Island. New York

Opposite page:
The entrance to the house leads into the passageway that connects the living section (left) to the bedrooms and children's bedrooms (right).

In November 1944 Bert Geller submitted a detailed list of what he wanted Breuer to include in the house. It foresaw a total of seven living and bedrooms, a spacious kitchen, a veranda, a double garage and a pantry. Presumably, a special permit had to be granted before beginning a house of this size in the spring or summer of 1945, since the war economy still placed restrictions on private building projects. For the Geller House, Breuer took recourse to a study that he had developed in 1943 to submit to a competition in an architectural magazine—where it had been deemed worthy of publication. A year later Breuer sent the design to a company in Boston interested in building inexpensive housing for its employees and received a rejection notice explaining that "our Editorial Board feels that our employees would not be sufficiently advanced to appreciate such an unusual style".

The main idea behind the study involved locating living spaces in two separate sections of the house according to their functions. The entrance, corridor, courtyard or terrace were located in between them. This so-called "bi-nuclear house" represents a logical continuation of the disposition of space developed by Breuer for the BAMBOS houses (where the studio and the living boxes had been separated) and for the Harnischmacher House (with the separate study). Thereafter, Breuer was to revert to this scheme often, sometimes with the two halves of the house laid out quite differently.

In the Geller House the bedrooms, children's bedrooms and a big central playroom for the children (with a large glass front facing south) are located in the larger, horizontally rectangular segment of the building, while the elongated rectangular part, running from back to front, housed the living and dining room along with the kitchen

The first fully developed design

View from the southwest
Both the living quarters on the right and the garage on the left have so-called butterfly roofs.

and a room for personnel. The two longer walls of the living area are completely glazed, and the fireplace is in the wall at the head of the room. Between the two sections, which have roofs pitched at opposing angles, forming a butterfly roof, there is an entrance and a veranda. The separate two-car garage, which includes a guest apartment, also has a butterfly roof creating a vibrant building ensemble. Breuer designed the plywood furniture for the light-coloured interior himself. In the playroom the doors were painted in bright blue, yellow and red—colours that remind one of De Stijl artworks, an accent that was henceforth often found in Breuer's homes.

At first, the distribution of the rooms seems completely logical, however it forces the complex daily routine of a family into a scheme that is far too simplistic. It is, for example, impossible for a mother to keep an eye on the children in the playroom while she is busy far away in the kitchen. Nevertheless, the popular magazine House & Architecture still called the Geller House "tomorrow's house today", and even in the 1960s many architects still made use of Breuer's bi-nuclear layout.

The large playroom is the central part of the wing for the bedrooms and children's bedrooms.

Floor plan

1947–1948 ▸ Breuer House II
New Canaan, Connecticut

View from the southeast

"In our modern houses the relationship to the landscape is a major planning element," Breuer wrote in 1955. "There are two entirely different approaches, and both may solve a problem well: there is the house that sits on the ground and permits you to walk outside at any point, from any room. This is a good solution, for children, in particular. And then there is the house on stilts, which is elevated above the surrounding landscape, almost like a camera on a tripod. This will give you a better view, almost a sensation of floating above the surroundings, or of standing on the bridge of a ship. It gives you a feeling of liberation, a certain élan, a certain daring .... My own favourite solution is the one that combines these two opposite sensations: the hillside house."

The second house that Breuer built for himself and his family was erected on the edge of a lawn property. The wooden living level is set on a raised concrete foundation that provides space for the children's bedroom. Most of the northern half of the living box, which projects as far as 9.8 feet beyond the foundation, is taken up by the main room: the living area, with a suspended veranda, the dining area, separated by a fireplace, and an entrance, separated by a three-quarter-height wall. The other rooms, the kitchen, the laundry, the bathroom and two bedrooms, can be reached through a narrow corridor along the back wall.

Shortly after construction began, Breuer departed on a trip to South America for several months leaving his employees to complete the house. They soon realized that Breuer's daring design for a house that would appear to be floating on air demanded too much of the wood-frame construction. "This is what you call an experiment" was all Breuer had to say on the matter in a letter from South America. But then he did express serious concern when not only the veranda, but also the corner of the living

This side view shows the walls that were added to support the extended balcony.
In 1986 Breuer's partner Herbert Beckhard added an extension to the back.

box began to sink. They were later supported by fieldstone walls to ensure their safety. Only four years later, Breuer built a bungalow with more characteristic fieldstone walls as a new home for himself and his family.

View to the dining area

View into the living area

Floor plan of the main level

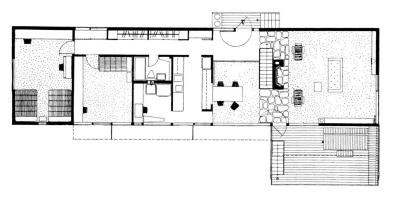

1948–1949 ▸ MoMA Research House
New York, New York

Opposite page:
The western part of the house from the south

The living room with a view into the bedroom on a higher level. The stairway is obscured by the wall of the fireplace.

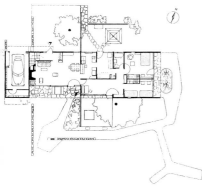

Floor plans

When the "House in the Museum Garden" was completed in the summer of 1949, it offered many visitors their first experience of modern residential architecture. This is precisely why the MoMA invited different architects to build a model house every year, starting in 1948. Breuer was the first to be honoured in this manner. His long narrow house is divided into four sections under a dramatic butterfly roof: the core of the house is the combined living and dining room, which opens up onto a recessed terrace and the garden through an extensively glazed front. The entrance to the house leads directly into this room, separated only by a wall of three-quarter height. An open stairway leads to the master bedroom, which is located over the garage and separated from the living room only by a curtain. It has a small recessed balcony with a stairway that leads directly into the garden. On the other side, a living room leads to an area with a kitchen, laundry, bathroom and children's playroom. Under the roof, which begins to rise again, there is a children's bedroom and a guestroom. Each of the two middle areas has its own courtyard off to the side, which is separated by walls and trellises: out front an entrance and a driveway, to the back a garden and play area with a sandpit.

The interior, which was only partially furnished by Breuer, made a very warm impression that contradicted the coolly impersonal, high-tech cliché of Modernism in which many people demanded. Breuer's house proved that it was possible to feel at home in modern architecture. However, at a price of $20,000 the house was much too expensive for a broad spectrum of the population. After the exhibition ended, the Rockefeller family bought the model house; today they use it as a guesthouse at their estate in Pocatino near New York.

1952 ▸ Caesar Cottage
Lakeville, Connecticut

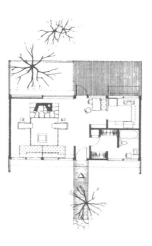

Floor plan

Right:
The entrance side

For years, Breuer kept a model of the little weekend house he built for Harry I. Caesar in 1952 on his desk—Breuer considered it one of his best designs. Again it consisted of a wooden box set on a raised fieldstone foundation. In this case, however, it extended so far out on three sides, as if truly floating, that it had to be shored up. The privacy of the rectangular house is protected by windowless walls that extend far beyond the back and front of the house on either side. The sides facing the woods and the lake, on the other hand, have ample fenestration. Set into the cubic form of the house is a veranda overlooking the lake and an area of open space cut out around a birch tree. The house is entered via a kind of gangway with tautly strung ropes as handrails. The "heart" of the house is a fireplace made of rusticated concrete with cylindrical draughts. The outer walls are clad with cypress boards, and the inner walls with walnut.

The open fireplace designed by Breuer

Opposite page:
The veranda

1952–1958 · UNESCO Headquarters

Paris, France

▸with Pier Luigi Nervi and Bernard Zehrfuss

The complex from the west with the high-rise secretariat building and the conference building to the right

The commission to build for the UNESCO (United Nations Educational, Scientific and Cultural Organization) headquarters in Paris catapulted Marcel Breuer, a specialist for residential projects on a regional level, into the top league of international star architects. Here again it was Walter Gropius who opened the door for him. Breuer told the following story: One afternoon in early 1952, the five architects who formed the advisory committee chaired by Gropius met in order to judge designs submitted by the French architect Eugène Baudin. None of them found them very good. So they went to a café on Boulevard Saint-Germain to put things in perspective. At that very moment Marcel Breuer came walking by. Breuer joined the group, and, after he left, Gropius suggested that they commission an international team made up of Breuer and two other architects. Perhaps it was not such a coincidence that Breuer was chosen, since Gropius was well aware of his ability to work within a team, and he was also able to tenaciously ward off attacks by Le Corbusier, who had wanted to build the complex himself. The trio consisted of the Frenchman Bernard Zehrfuss and the Italian engineer Pier Luigi Nervi, who was famous for his façades and exterior designs. Breuer's main responsibility consisted of designing the façades and the outer areas. He was later to describe the cooperation with Nervi as the most fruitful he ever experienced.

After drafting a highly controversial design for a different building site (at Porte Maillot), "BNZ" designed the tripartite complex that was erected at Place de Fontenoy in the Seventh Arrondissement in 1955–1958. It consists of an eight-storey secretariat building with a "Y" shaped footprint, a conference building laid out in the shape of a trapeze, and a five-storey office building with a square floor plan behind it. The ensemble is arranged on spacious grounds, which feature a reclining figure by Henry Moore and two murals by Joan Miró. Originally accessible to the public, the entire complex is now protected by walls and fences. The entrance is through what is actually

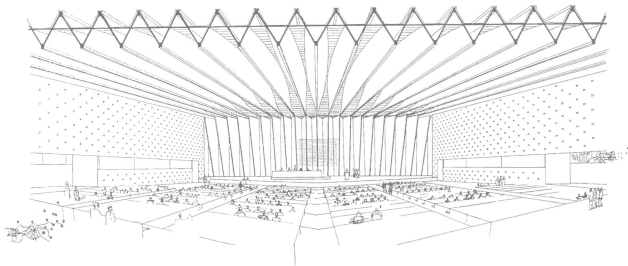

Drawing of the assembly hall in the
conference building

Right:
The rear façade of the conference building

Opposite page:
Foyer of the secretariat

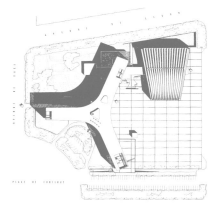

Floor plan of the first two building segments, before the construction of the smaller office building

the back of the high-rise building. Zehrfuss added building IV on the grounds in 1965. It has two floors below street level, with daylight provided through six inner courtyards.

The high-rise building, with 800 offices, rests on 72 supports. The ground level area originally had glazing all around the 23-foot high, slanted concrete piers. All of the external walls on the upper floors are non-supporting, curtain wall façades. The three front walls are clad in travertine, the long sides are fully glazed to the east and south west; the northern façade is clad in travertine with horizontal windows in a staggered pattern. For each of the directions in which the windows face, there are four different types of solar protection systems. The main façade has a lively relief created by solar protection in the form of concrete grids, travertine blinds, metal bars and solar glass.

A low-rise middle section, called the "Salle des Pas Perdus", connects the high-rise building with the conference centre, with a large and small hall, reception rooms and offices. Its front and butterfly roof are made of folded reinforced concrete. Nervi wanted to limit this effect to the roof, but Breuer argued in favour of using it for the concrete façade as well, a motif that he would use again for other buildings. The long sides feature polished travertine, rough granite and areas of glass—and are therefore typical of the overall complex, the fascination of which is derived from the contrasting forms and materials.

1953–1961 ▸ St. John's Abbey and University
Collegeville, Minnesota ▸ Library with Hamilton P. Smith

Opposite page:
Stairway to the freestanding gallery

The church and the campanile from the northeast

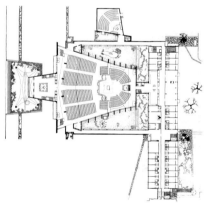

Floor plan of the church and the living quarters

The construction and expansion of the largest Benedictine abbey in the world, and the university associated with it, progressed in phases, ultimately becoming one of Marcel Breuer's most successful projects. Based on a master plan drawn up in 1953, he built a new dormitory wing for the monks, a church, two student dormitories, a library, a natural science department and an institute for ecumenical research over a period of a decade and a half. They either augmented or replaced older Neo-Romanesque buildings.

The abbot, Baldwin Dworschak, wrote a letter to twelve famous architects, stating that: "We feel that the modern architect with his orientation towards functionalism and honest use of materials is uniquely qualified to produce a Catholic building." Later the abbot said that they chose in favour of Breuer because of his personality, modesty, his honesty and because he was a good listener, who the monks felt took their wishes and needs seriously. For his part, Breuer was deeply impressed by the lives of the monks, their seriousness and humanism.

The new monastery building took on a model character. Intended as a demonstration of what modern church architecture should look like, it was to provide an adequate architectural expression of the feeling of community within this reform-oriented abbey. The first building, completed in 1954–1955, was a three-storey residential wing, based on modules measuring twelve-by-twelve feet. It is not a spectacular building, but one that was to prove itself in everyday life. Breuer benefited from the faith the monks had in him in executing this spectacular church begun in 1958 and consecrated three years later. The church is trapezoidal both in floor plan and elevation and becomes lower and narrower towards the wall behind the altar. The side walls and the ceiling feature the

View of the church's interior from the gallery

same folding technique used for the conference buildings at the UNESCO Headquarters, and Breuer actually called in Pier Luigi Nervi as a consultant on the plans for St. John's. The interior, which is free of internal supports and offers seating for 1,700 people in the nave, on the freestanding gallery and on the horseshoe-shaped benches of the choir, is illuminated by low windows and an amber-coloured skylight over the altar and through the northern wall. The latter has windows embedded in a concrete structure made up of 540 hexagons.

In front of the fully glazed north side of the church—which is half the height again of the low porch with a baptistery—a 98-foot bell tower in the form of a wide, trapezoidal sail made of concrete rises. It is perforated to provide space for a cross and five bells. The sail has four supports reminiscent of the base of the Eiffel Tower. Breuer actually did change the original plan after working on the UNESCO project in Paris in 1956, from which he had a view of the Eiffel Tower. The campanile reminded Breuer of

The reading room of the library

the banners carried out in front of church processions. The sail was originally conceived to reflect the sun, in order to direct as much light as possible into the church through the windows facing north.

The library was built in 1964–1966, a granite-clad rectangular building that makes a subdued impression from outside. Inside, it has two storeys with high ceilings, the lower of which is mainly below ground, a central stairway connects the two. There are no windows in the outer walls below the upper half of the top floor, i.e. up to the top of the bookshelves. The wall area above is completely glazed and protected from the sun by hollow bricks installed on three sides. The ceiling is supported by an impressive structure: two concrete columns that fan out in eight directions like the branches of a tree.

1954–1963 · Annunciation Priory of the Sisters of St. Benedict

Bismarck, North Dakota ▸ with Hamilton P. Smith

The inner courtyard formed by the rooms used communally by the nuns

Through the good offices of St. John's Abbey, Breuer received a commission from the Benedictine nuns in Bismarck, North Dakota in 1954. They wanted to build a priory on a barren plateau overlooking the Missouri River Valley, seven miles outside of the city. This second of Breuer's three great monastic buildings was completed in two stages. It was begun in 1958 as a flat "island" in the virtually interminable vastness of the prairie. It is overshadowed by a 98-foot campanile that is reminiscent of a ship's mast with a hoisted sail into which an enormous cross—which is visible from far and wide—was cut. However, it is not located at the centre of the rectangular compound, but rather out in front of it, aligned with the chapel. It is a masterpiece of modern concrete architecture—the relief-like structure of the surface was created solely by the way the form boards were arranged before the concrete was poured.

The priory complex forms an elongated rectangle in which four parallel building sections are integrated: from west to east there is a three-storey residential wing forming one narrow side of the rectangle, the chapel, a section with rooms for dining, recreation and seminars for Mary College, and the living quarters for the students on a second narrow side. The building segments are connected by inner courtyards and a pair of two-storey walkways. To the south, the ensemble is framed by an open passageway that rests on V-shaped supports. Outside of the rectangle, behind the priory a building with additional rooms for joint use by the nuns has been added. The façades of the living quarters are divided into squares, the fields of which alternately contain windows or are filled in with brick. Otherwise, exposed concrete and granite are the dominant materials. The dynamic roofscape of the chapel was created by using hyperbolic paraboloids. In 1965–1968, separate classrooms and dormitories were built for Mary College, a short distance away.

1956–1961▸New York University Buildings

New York, New York

▸with Hamilton P. Smith

Opposite page:
Begrisch Hall from the west

Begrisch Hall in front of the student union (semi-obscured) and the dormitory

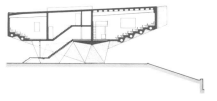

North-south cross section

Breuer and his partners extended the historic University Heights Campus (now Bronx Community College) by adding four buildings on a site that sloped steeply (down to the Harlem River): a five-storey technical institute, a small lecture hall, a low-rise student union which included a dining hall, and a seven-storey dormitory. The dormitory provided a barrier to the drop through its elongated, angular floor plan. In 1967–1970 a second building for laboratories and classrooms was added as a high-rise complex with a façade made of prefabricated concrete elements.

The gem in this ensemble is the small building with two lecture halls, which is now called *Begrisch Hall* (in honour of the sponsor). It seems unusual between the generously fenestrated, light-coloured façades of Breuer's other buildings. Breuer's idea was to remove the lecture halls from the institute buildings and put them in a separate building. From the outside it reminds one of a solid block of concrete, like a sea-saw that is artfully balanced on two supports under the side walls. Those who dare can park their cars under it. The walls are only perforated by a few small windows, which provide no indication of how space is distributed inside. Seams in the masonry delineate a series of differently sized, asymmetric fields, each with a different pattern produced by the form boards.

The building has two lecture halls, with rows of seats set on tiers reflected in the staggered underside of the building. In the middle there is a stairway, some small functional rooms and a foyer, from which a bridge leads over to the neighbouring institute.

1957–1959 · Hooper House II
Towson near Baltimore, Maryland

Opposite page:
The garden side from the northeast

Only a few years after creating a very daring structure for his own home in New Canaan, Breuer built a bungalow for himself and his family in 1951. Its flat roof rested on what appeared to be solid walls, which were clad in large blocks of fieldstone. This is the type of house that inspired the one Breuer designed for the Hoopers in 1957, and which was built in a northern suburb of Baltimore by 1959. (Breuer had already planned the renovation and expansion of their former, more traditional, house in 1949.) This second Hooper House is located on a park-like site, and offers a view of a lake through the windows facing east. The New Canaan house owned by Breuer's short-time partner Eliot Noyes, which Edith Hooper greatly admired, served as a model. Making use of some of Breuer's ideas, Noyes had used an inner courtyard to separate the living and dining areas, and simple fieldstone walls for the long sides of the bungalow. The original model can still be recognized in the Hooper House, but some decisive modifications were undertaken.

The massive, 131-foot-long fieldstone wall on the western side of the house has an opening from floor to ceiling in the middle, creating an entrance that is covered by a flat canopy. It leads into the hallway between the two parts of the house: the bedrooms, children's bedrooms and the guestroom lie to the left; the living room, dining room and kitchen to the right. An inner courtyard separates the two parts. The rooms open onto the garden, to the east, through floor-to-ceiling windows with sliding glass doors. Atypically, the glazing is not interrupted by walls or window frames, except for a fieldstone wall at the centre, parallel to the courtyard. It in turn has a large, rectangular opening that creates an interesting effect: from the front entrance it is possible to look through the double glass doors, the glass wall of the hallway, the inner courtyard, and the opening in the eastern wall and to see the landscape behind the house, without seeing any of the rooms themselves. The solid western wall has one drawback: the only natural light in the adjoining kitchen is through skylights. This also holds true for the

Elevation of the northern façade with the two divergent levels

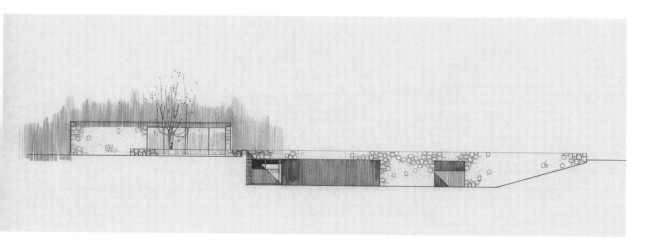

children's playroom, which is located at the interface between the western wall (stairway to the lower level) and the, also windowless, northern wall of the atrium. The garage and some small functional rooms are located on the lower level. It is open to the north, since the site drops off slightly. This lower level is set off to the northwest of the house itself, to which it is connected by a stairway and passageway. Relatively austere and abstract in its composition, the Hooper house is made more vibrant by the interaction between interior and exterior spaces, as well as the views of the landscape—and, not least of all, by the exciting contrast between the great areas of glass and the carefully textured fieldstone walls.

Opposite page, above:
Playroom with fireplace

Opposite page, below:
Floor plan

View of the courtyard from the living room
The entrance to the house can be seen on the left.

The atrium from the hallway

1960–1962 · IBM Research Centre
La Gaude near Nice, France ▸ with Robert F. Gatje

Aerial view from the east

Breuer's partner Robert F. Gatje told the story of a shared taxi ride through Manhattan. When they passed the Whitney Museum Breuer said: "I know most people think the Whitney is my most successful building, but my personal favourite is La Gaude."

The IBM Research Centre north of Nice marks a pivotal point in Breuer's oeuvre. The clients wanted a building that provided a great deal of space, but was no more than three storeys tall, to avoid long trips in lifts. It also had to satisfy French building laws requiring daylight for every workplace. This inevitably resulted in long, narrow wings with single corridors, which Breuer arranged in the form of a double "Y". Breuer liked the open, inviting gesture of wide stretched wings and also argued that it prevented employees from looking into each other's windows.

His love of concrete and the need to protect the offices from the heat of the sun in southern France, inspired Breuer to create a revolutionary façade: he designed a system of concrete modules that supported the weight of the roof and served as solar protection. They were so voluminous that they provided space to install air conditioning, electrical wiring and the like. They project out about 3 feet beyond the windows of the IBM building. The width of the modules, 6 feet, reflects IBM's planning grid, which was aimed at maintaining flexibility inside of the building. All the internal walls, with the exception of the stairways, lifts and bathrooms, are made of wood. In order to save time and money, the prefabricated façade segments were made off-site.

The uneven, rocky building site led Breuer to develop a second innovation: he set the two office and laboratory levels on tree-like, forking concrete supports, which were

The entire building rests on heavy, three-pronged, concrete supports.
Unlike the impression created by the tri-partite front, the inside of the building can be used variably on both levels.

poured on-site because of their different heights. Breuer wanted to put the main entrance on ground level between the two supports, but IBM insisted on a more impressive entrance up a level higher, so Breuer designed a ramp as a driveway leading up to the main entrance.

The facility proved to be so practical that two major extensions were added by 1978, and Breuer built a similar facility for IBM in Boca Raton, Florida, in 1968–1972, grouping three double "Ys" around an artificial lake.

Breuer used façade systems made of deep, highly structured concrete modules for several building commissions after that. Buildings with façades made of prefabricated segments could be erected fast and economically, and many clients approached him for this very reason. These somewhat similar yet always unique façades characterized much of Breuer's late work and made him one of the most commercially successful architects of the 1960s and early 1970s. Unfortunately, they also tarnished his reputation in the eyes of architectural critics. One should, however, be fair enough to admit that the physical quality of this architecture, its unique and fascinating expressivity, and the high degree of care for detail cannot be understood by viewing photographs.

1960–1966 ▸ St. Francis de Sales Church

Muskegon, Michigan ▸ with Herbert Beckhard

View from the northeast

Breuer once said that he would have been even more famous if his best buildings hadn't all been at the end of the world. His third major ecclesiastical project was also erected far from any major city, on the eastern shore of Lake Michigan. The St. Francis de Sales Church is the most expressive of all of Breuer's buildings—a sculpture in concrete rising to a height of 98 feet, completely windowless, with only the pattern of the form boards structuring the extensive wall surfaces. The highly idiosyncratic volume of the church rises from a rectangular footprint: the side walls twist in the form of a hyperbolic paraboloid making the trapezoidal front of the church wider at the top, while the back becomes narrower. The front and back walls lean inward slightly. The church bells hang above the façade in a concrete trough that runs the full length of the roof, also providing space for air conditioning. Leaving the walled forecourt, the church is entered through a low vestibule, with a baptistery and the confessionals, before reaching the nave with seating for 1,700. It seems archaic: the roof, altar and west wall are structured and reinforced by concrete ribs with the only daylight filtering in through the skylights in the roof. Above the altar to the left there is a chapel for the Blessed Sacrament, the two walls of which form an angle that juts out of the back wall of the church. At the back of the nave a freestanding gallery rests on wedge-shaped concrete supports. The side walls are covered with white plaster panels for acoustic purposes, the flooring is the same polished red brick as at St. John's. As in all of his churches, Breuer designed the altar, the baptismal font and the choir stands himself.

Opposite page:
The interior

1960–1976 › Ski Resort

Flaine, France › with Robert F. Gatje

Opposite page:
Panorama of the entire ensemble

The Hotel Le Flaine protrudes considerably over the cliff.

Breuer had the chance to plan an entire city twice: the ski resort Flaine in the French Alps in 1960, and the satellite city for 15,000 residents near Bayonne in southwestern France in 1964. Altogether Breuer completed a total of six projects in France, more than in any other country besides the United States. He was, however, only able to procure a licence to practise architecture in France after long negotiations, since his never having completed formal training, let alone a degree programme in architecture, proved detrimental. Only in June 1964 was he allowed to open his own office in Paris, yet Breuer had already been commuting between New York and his self-proclaimed favourite city of Paris for several years.

The ski resort planned for 6,000 guests was created in an alpine valley at an elevation of 6,000 feet, which was previously only accessible on foot, southeast of Geneva near the motorway to Chamonix. In the 1950s, a consortium of private investors had secured the rights to build on the site; one of them was a brother of one of the Breuers' neighbours in New Canaan. In 1960 this neighbour and friend asked whether Breuer would be interested in drawing up a master plan and the architect quickly agreed, since he had already designed a ski hotel in Obergurgl in Tyrol in 1937–1938, which he was no longer able to realize after Austria's annexation by Germany.

By the time Breuer became involved, plans on how to access the valley had made great progress. It was also already clear that the buildings were to be built out of glass and prefabricated concrete parts. The latter were produced far below in the Arve Valley

and transported up to Flaine using a specially constructed gondola. In laying out the town itself, Breuer adhered to a few basic principles. On his first visit to the town by helicopter in 1960 he said: "We must not spoil the site." For him that meant that the town should not be extended any further than necessary and that the building volume should be concentrated on the least number of structures possible. The second basic idea was to bundle automobile traffic: the access road ends in the middle of the town at a large car park, from which all of the buildings can be reached on foot. A third basic principle also contributed to the compact nature of the town: the visitors were to be able to reach the central lift station quickly and comfortably on foot from their accommodation with their skis on their shoulders. Breuer had a big model of the valley measuring 6 by 4 feet constructed for his office, which he used to arrange the building masses again and again, using building blocks, until he found a final solution.

In 1961 Breuer drew up the master plan, parallel to the construction of the access road. In two construction phases, 1961–1968 and 1974–1976, the town was built on four levels on the sunny north side of the valley—with a view of the ski slopes to the east and south. At the centre, all very close together, there were cafés, shops, a church, a school, a cinema, a skating rink, a swimming pool and tennis courts. The flat residential buildings, as well as the multi-storey hotels and apartment buildings, are located overlooking the centre, arranged in rows, each of which can be reached via an access road. Each of the hotels built in the first phase is connected to an apartment building, so that the residents of the apartments could use the restaurants in the corresponding

Hotel lobby with a fireplace custom-designed by Breuer

hotels and deposit their keys there. All of the buildings, the flat ones as well as the high-rise edifices, were constructed using prefabricated concrete elements; however the façades exhibit very different structures. Photographs of the hotel "Le Flaine", which juts far out over a cliff on its narrow side, have often been published.

The official opening of Flaine was Christmas 1968, although many areas were still under construction. In 1976 the last buildings, the church and a hotel at the centre of the town, were finally finished. Because of the short distances and the child-oriented, auto-free layout of the centre, Flaine soon became a successful ski resort.

1963–1966 ▸ Koerfer House
Moscia, Switzerland ▸ with Herbert Beckhard

Opposite page, above:
View from the east

View from the dining area into the living area, which is a few steps away from the open study, where a door leads into the master bedroom.

Floor plan

"This is going to be my last guest appearance in Switzerland," Breuer wrote to a friend in frustration over the Doldertal Houses in 1935. Fortunately, he later broke this vow, creating two of his most beautiful villas in Switzerland. The Villa Staehelin, overlooking Lake Zurich, was built in 1957–1958, and the house he created for factory owner and art collector Jacques Koerfer, high above Lago Maggiore, in 1963–1966. When Breuer suggested a concrete shell roof, Koerfer said he "would prefer the simplest solution over anything complicated ... but to my mind that needn't exclude a more open, inspired floor plan with inner courtyards and interior gardens or even a two-storey floor plan".

Breuer ultimately designed a spacious, three-storey compound. The lower level, part of which projects from the sloping site, provides space for garages and rooms for personnel. The living room and the bedrooms are on the nearly square main floor, surrounded by a broad lawn, shored up by walls. The smaller upper floor—with three children's bedrooms, a playroom and a guest room—is extended on three sides by using the roof of the main floor as a terrace.

Most of the main floor is taken up by a large room, which extends from front to back with various elements used as room-dividers defining different areas; only the bedrooms are really separate. The house is accessed via a ramp between a cliff and the back of the house to leading to a small forecourt. After entering through the back, a spacious gallery leads to the living room with a panoramic view of the lake, through large windows, and the very substantial cubic furniture that Breuer designed for the house. The surfaces of the walls, columns and balusters are made of granite and concrete that displays rough traces of form boards and hammering.

1963–1966 ▸ Whitney Museum of American Art

New York, New York ▸ with Hamilton P. Smith

The exhibition space on the third floor with the only window overlooking Madison Avenue

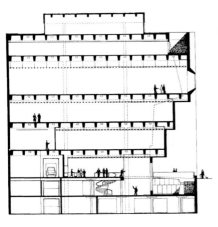

East-west cross section

Opposite page:
View from the northwest
Two slabs of concrete separate the museum from the neighbouring buildings.

"What should a museum look like, a museum in Manhattan? ... It is easier to say first what it should not look like. It should not look like a business or an office building, nor should it look like a place of light entertainment. Its form and its material should have identity and weight in the neighbourhood of fifty-storey skyscrapers, of mile-long bridges, in the midst of the dynamic jungle of our colourful city. It should be an independent and a self-reliant unit, exposed to history, and at the same time it should have visual connection to the street, as deemed fitting for housing twentieth-century art. It should transform the vitality of the street into the sincerity and profundity of art." Thus began the text Breuer submitted with his proposal for the Whitney Museum of American Art, a building destined to become his most famous. On a relatively small corner site, measuring 98 by 125 feet, Breuer created a building that is clearly distinguished from those surroundings it and also works well as a museum.

The clients wanted a highly flexible exhibition space, so Breuer designed three exhibition levels with ceilings between 13 and 17 feet, few windows and no internal supports. Smaller areas serve to display the permanent collection. Prefabricated concrete grids suspended from the ceilings allow lighting and partitions to be installed variably. The design of the rooms is subtle, the walls and ceilings are predominantly grey with dark grey slate flooring. The entrance hall is located on the ground floor, with a cafeteria and museum shop on a lower level. The dense grid of light-reflecting, concave aluminium discs suspended from the ceiling gives the entrance hall its character.

A second level below ground, not accessible to the public, serves as a vault. The offices on the top floor are illuminated by daylight. In between the top floor and the closed front of the building is a roof garden.

On the Madison Avenue side, the building's mass is staggered, projecting further out from floor to floor. The sculpture garden, below street level between the pavement and the building, is traversed by a bridge protected by a concrete canopy. It can be accessed through a wall of glass that divides the sculpture garden into an outer and an inner area. The remainder of the cube is faced with grey granite and has only seven windows to the outside world. One window (like the eye of a Cyclops) is on the upper exhibition level facing Madison Avenue, the remaining six appear to be arbitrarily scattered on the straight wall that faces East 75th Street. The windows are set in frames that look almost like a pyramid sheared off at an angle. On Madison Avenue the museum is set off from the next building, the gap being filled by a recessed stairway; firewalls made of exposed concrete emphasize the museum's solitary character. According to Breuer: "This all serves to transform the building into a sculpture itself."

The sculpture garden
Outdoor and indoor spaces interlock with the many different levels to create an exciting panoply.

Opposite page:
Staggering the façade created space for the sculpture garden a level below.

1967–1969 ▸ Geller House II
Lawrence, Long Island, New York
▸ with Herbert Beckhard

View from the southeast

After the mid-1950s Breuer built very few private residences. He did, however, remain loyal to some of his old clients. Hence, in 1967, he accepted a commission from the Gellers who had been among his first clients when he worked as an independent architect in New York. They agreed to let Breuer use a design that was planned (but never built) as a holiday home for a wealthy industrialist in the ski resort of Aspen (Colorado) in 1959. The layout of the house, which is nearly perfectly square, is concealed under a parabolically arched shell. The southern half, with an ocean view, is taken up by a single room that serves as a living room, dining room and kitchen—the kitchen appliances are located on the narrow side of the room. The living and dining room are not separated by a room divider, as is generally the case in Breuer's houses, but by virtue of the fact that the seating area in front of the fireplace is sunken. The northern half of the building has two storeys. On the ground floor there are three bedrooms and a dressing room. On the upper level there is a large study and a sauna. Walls protect the privacy of the entrance courtyard and the terrace. The garden side, oriented to the south, is completely glazed behind a geometric grid of deep concrete elements that provide solar protection.

Opposite page:
The big living room with the kitchen area, dining table and sunken seating area in front of the fireplace

1967–1970 ▸ Cleveland Museum of Art
Cleveland, Ohio ▸ with Hamilton P. Smith

View of the entrance façade from the east

The success of the Whitney Museum led to Breuer's being commissioned to design an extension to the Cleveland Museum of Art as an additional wing with space for classrooms, an auditorium and a special exhibition area. While the New York museum had a total of seven windows, in Cleveland Marcel Breuer decided to do without daylight altogether. The new building is divided into cubes of various sizes, reflecting their internal uses. The large wall areas are enlivened by bands of light and dark granite. The cathedral in the Italian town of Orvieto that Breuer greatly admired probably served as a model. The new building is closely aligned with an old wing of the museum. While its exterior provides a stark contrast to the Beaux-Arts façade of the 1916 building, the interior adheres to the ceiling height of the older building.

In Cleveland Breuer was able to further develop the concrete canopies that were so typical of his later work, creating a long one supported by two pairs of columns, under which visitors could make their way from the car park into the entrance hall of the new museum building. From here a path leads straight to the old building, to an auditorium with 770 seats on the right, or, upstairs to the left, to special exhibition spaces without internal supports, to provide more flexibility in hanging shows. The ceilings of the halls are, as in the Whitney Museum, made of suspended concrete grids that enable lighting and partitions to be easily rearranged. The classrooms are located on the lower level, where there is also a sunken courtyard similar to the one that was so successful in New York.

Perspective drawing of the entrance side

1972–1973 ▸ Saier House

Glanville, France ▸ with Mario Jossa

From the north, the lower level with the bedrooms is visible. The kitchen can be found above, in the corner on the right.

Opposite page:
View of the entrance to the main house from the annex, through the courtyard

For his only residential structure in France, Marcel Breuer again decided to rework an older design for a house that had never been built. Because he had been so impressed by the villa Breuer built for lawyer Wilhelm Staehelin, overlooking Lake Zurich, Peter Ustinov asked Breuer to build him a house near Vevey on Lake Geneva in 1959. Breuer came up with different designs for a "quadro-nuclear" house which included a living cell covered by a roof formed by two concrete hyperbolic paraboloids. At that time Breuer was building a library for Hunter College in the Bronx with a floor plan measuring 120 by 180 feet spanned by a dynamic roofscape of hyperbolic paraboloids—a construction that had only seldom been used outside of Latin America up to that point. Breuer's former student Eduardo Catalano had built a house with that kind of roof for himself in the United States. Breuer was fascinated by it and used the construction several times after that. The Ustinov project was never executed for reasons of cost, and two other attempts to build a residence with a concrete shell roof failed to be realized—once because of the client's taste, the second time because of the cost.

In 1972 the Saiers saw the blueprint for the Ustinov house, a blueprint which was used

Floor plan of the main level

to decorate a display of some furniture by Breuer in a shop in Paris. They contacted Breuer's Paris office, of which Mario Jossa was then the director, and in 1972–1973 the house was built near Deauville, with a view of the sea. At the request of Saier's wife, the walls were made of light-coloured concrete, so that they would not seem menacing under the often cloudy sky of Normandy.

The Saier House consists of two living cells that are only connected by a wall—on the west side there is an open courtyard, on the east side a terrace with a swimming pool. The big living room/dining room area, including a fireplace and a kitchen, is located under the impressive roof, which is supported by three columns, and its external walls, which are almost completely glazed. A stairway leads to the bedrooms on a lower level, which is partially concealed behind a man-made wall of earth. The second living cell, one-storey with a flat roof, contains three additional bedrooms, a small inner courtyard and the garage.

Life and Work

The dates cited indicate when the planning began and not when the buildings were completed.

1902 ▶ Marcel Lajos Breuer was born as the son of dentist Jakob Breuer, 35, and his wife Franciska, 30, in the town of Pécs (Hungary). He was the youngest of their three children. A copy of the entry in the registry of births, found among his effects, indicates his birthday as May 21. However, May 22 is also often cited.

1920 ▶ After completing his school exams, Breuer enrolled himself at the Academy of Fine Arts in Vienna full scholarship. After just a few weeks, he applied to the Bauhaus in Weimar.

1920–1924 ▶ Breuer completed the Basic Course and an apprenticeship as a cabinetmaker. He soon abandoned painting totally. In 1923 he began to draft architectural designs, which were never implemented.

1924 ▶ After his journeyman's exam, Breuer spent a few months in Paris.

1925 ▶ Breuer became one of the young masters and directed the furniture workshop at the Bauhaus, which had moved to Dessau by that point. He experimented with a new material, tubular steel, designing his famous tubular steel furniture in the following three years.

1926 ▶ Breuer married Bauhaus student Martha Erps. They were divorced in 1934.

1927 ▶ In order to produce and market his tubular steel furniture in series, Breuer founded the Standard-Möbel furniture company in Berlin with a partner from Hungary.

1928 ▶ Breuer left the Bauhaus and opened an architectural office of his own in Berlin. He took part in competitions for major projects and designed interiors for wealthy patrons of the arts, particularly in Berlin.

1931 ▶ Breuer embarked on a long automobile tour through Southern Europe and Morocco, accompanied by his Bauhaus colleague Herbert Bayer. While he was travelling, he received his first

The young Marcel Breuer in St. Elme, France, 1928

building commission from a Wiesbaden industrialist.

1932
Harnischmacher House I, Wiesbaden, Germany

1933 ▶ Breuer left Germany and opened an architectural office in Budapest with two colleagues.
Doldertal Houses, Zurich, Switzerland

1934 ▶ At the Museum for Arts and Crafts in Zurich, Breuer formulated his architectural credo in the lecture "Wo stehen wir heute?" (Where do we stand today?).
Spring Trade Fair 1935, Budapest, Hungary

1935 ▶ Breuer relocated to London and entered into a partnership with the young architect F.R.S. Yorke. Breuer designed plywood furniture for a company called Isokon, did interior design work, but had almost no opportunity to build anything.

1936
Gane's Pavilion, Bristol, Great Britain
London Theatre Studio, London, Great Britain
Rose House (Shangri-La), Lee-on-Solent,

Opposite page:
Marcel Breuer, around 1949

Marcel Breuer in front of the Geller House I

Hampshire, Great Britain
Sea Lane House, Angmering-on-Sea, Sussex, Great Britain

1937 ▶ At the invitation of Walter Gropius, Breuer went to the United States. He taught at Harvard University in Cambridge near Boston (in the capacity of an associate professor after 1939) and established a joint architectural practice with Gropius. By 1941 they had realized ten buildings.
Hagerty House, Cohasset, Mass.
Gropius House, Lincoln, Mass.

1938
Two Houses for Masters, Eton College, Willowbrook, Great Britain
Wheaton College Art Center, Norton, Mass.
Breuer House I, Lincoln, Mass.
Fischer House, New Hope, Pa.
Frank House, Pittsburgh, Pa.

1939
Ford House, Lincoln, Mass.
Pennsylvania State Exhibition, World's Fair, New York, N.Y.

1940 ▶ Breuer married his secretary, Constance (Connie) Leighton. They had a son, Tamas (Tom), and adopted a three-year-old girl from Germany in 1959, Francesca (Cesca).
Weizenblatt House, Asheville, N.C.
Chamberlain Cottage, Wayland, Mass.
Abelle House, Framingham, Mass.

1941 ▶ A rift developed between Breuer and Gropius, which did not cause long-term damage to their friendship. Breuer worked as a freelance architect. He developed model solutions for prefabricated and single-family homes.
Aluminium City Terrace, New Kensington, Pa.

1944 ▶ Breuer became a United States citizen.
Geller House I, Lawrence, N.Y.

1945
Tompkins House, Hewlett Harbor, N.Y.

1946 ▶ Breuer took a sabbatical from Harvard and opened an office on East 88th Street in Manhattan. He decided not to return to the university. Breuer was soon in great demand as a residential architect among New York families looking to move to the country.
Fischer House, guest cottage, New Hope, Pa.
Robinson House, Williamstown, Mass.

1947 ▶ In the autumn, Breuer left for an extended lecture tour of South America. He declined an offer to establish a school of architecture in Buenos Aires.
Thompson House, Ligonier, Pa.
Breuer House II, New Canaan, Conn.
Scott House, Dennis, Mass.
Mills House, New Canaan, Conn.
Ariston Club, Mar del Plata, Argentina
Kniffin House, New Canaan, Conn.

1948
Kepes Cottage, Wellfleet, Mass.
Breuer Cottage, Wellfleet, Mass.
Witalis House, King's Point, N.Y.
MoMA Research House, New York, N.Y.
Hooper House I, Baltimore, Md.

1949
Airport Terminal Buildings, Fairbanks and Anchorage, Alaska
Rand House, Harrison, N.Y.
Potter House, Cape Elizabeth, Maine
Herrick House, Canajoharie, N.Y.
Tilley House, Middletown, Red Bank, N.J.
Marshad House, Croton-on-Hudson, N.Y.
Wolfson Trailer House, Pleasant Valley, N.Y.
Foote House, Chappaqua, N.Y.
Smith House, Aspen, Colo.
Clark House, Orange, Conn.

1950
Lauck House, Princeton, N.J.
Pack House, Scarsdale, N.Y.
Englund House, Pleasantville, N.Y.

Stillman House I, Litchfield, Conn.
Vassar College Dormitory, Poughkeepsie, N.Y.
McComb House, Poughkeepsie, N.Y.
Hanson House, Huntington, N.Y.

1951
Breuer House III, New Canaan, Conn.
S. Lawrence College Art Center, Bronxville, N.Y.
Grosse Pointe Public Library, Grosse Pointe, Mich.
Abraham & Strauss Department Store, Exterior, Hempstead, N.Y.

1952
Caesar Cottage, Lakeville, Conn.
Levy House, Princeton, N.J.
Torrington Company, Oakville, Ontario, Canada
UNESCO Headquarters, Paris, France

1953
Northfield Elementary School, Litchfield, Conn.
Aufricht House addition, Mamaroneck, N.Y.
Neumann House, Croton-on-Hudson, N.Y.
Snower House, Kansas City, Kans.
Edgar Stillmann Jr. Cottage, Wellfleet, Mass.
Harnischmacher House II, Wiesbaden, Germany
St John's Abbey and University, Collegeville, Minn.
De Bijenkorf Department Store, Rotterdam, The Netherlands

1954
Grieco House, Andover, Mass.
O. E. McIntyre Inc., Westbury, N.Y.
Starkey/Alworth House, Duluth, Minn.
Litchfield High School, Litchfield, Conn.
Bantam Elementary School, Bantam, Conn.
Annuciation Priory of the Sisters of St. Benedict, Bismarck, N.D.

1955
Connecticut Junior Republic, Litchfield, Conn.
Karsten House, Owings Mill, Md.
Torrington Company, Van Nuys, Calif.
Laaff House, Andover, Mass.
Institute for Advanced Study Housing, Princeton, N.J.

1956
Gagarin House I, Litchfield, Conn.
United States Embassy, The Hague, The Netherlands
New York University Buildings, New York, N.Y.
Staehelin House, Feldmeilen/Zurich, Switzerland

1957
Van Leer Vatenfabrieken Office Building,

Marcel Breuer in front of the bell tower of St. John's University

Amstelveen, The Netherlands
Krieger House, Bethesda, Md.
Hooper House II, Towson/Baltimore, Md.
Westchester Synagogue, Scarsdale, N.Y.
Hunter College Library, New York, N.Y.

1959
Torrington Company, Rochester, Ind.

1960
McMullen Beach House, Mantoloking, N.J.
Halverson Fishing Camp, Dryberry Lake Island, Ontario, Canada
IBM Research Center, La Gaude/Nice, France
St. Francis de Sales Church, Muskegon, Mich.
Flaine Ski Resort, Flaine, France

1961
Kacmarcik House, St. Paul, Minn.
Breuer Cottage, studio, Wellfleet, Mass.

1962
Torrington Company, Machine Building, Torrington, Conn.

1963
Wise House, Wellfleet, Mass.
Fairview Heights Apartments, Ithaca, N.Y.
Torrington Company, Nivelles, Belgium
Koerfer House, Moscia, Switzerland
Whitney Museum of American Art, New York, N.Y.
Department of Housing and Urban Development, Washington, D.C.
ZUP Development, Bayonne, France

1964 ▶ Breuer opened an office in Paris; Herbert Beckhard, Murray Emsley (for one year), Robert F. Gatje and Hamilton P. Smith became equal partners; in 1974 Tician Papachristou joined them.
Stillman House II, Litchfield, Conn.
Torrington Company, Swindon, England

1965
Sarget-Ambrine, Office Building and Laboratory, Merignac, France
Torrington Company Administration Building, Torrington, Conn.

1966
Yale University Engineering Building, New Haven, Conn.

1967
Roxbury Campus High School, Boston, Mass.
Geller House II, Lawrence, N.Y.
University Heights Technology Building II, New York, N.Y.
Cleveland Museum of Art, Cleveland, Ohio
Armstrong Rubber Company Headquarters, West Haven, Conn.
Convent of the Sisters of Devine Providence, Baldegg, Switzerland
Department of Health, Education and Welfare, Washington, D.C.

1968
IBM Research Center first expansion, La Gaude/Nice, France
IBM Administrative, Laboratory and Manufacturing Facility, Boca Raton, Fla.
Grand Coulee Dam, Third Power Plant and Forebay Dam, Grand Coulee, Wash.

1970
De Bijenkorf Department Store, Parking Garage, Rotterdam, The Netherlands

1971
Torrington Corporation, Technical Center, Torrington, Conn.
Bryn Mawr Lower and Elementary School, Baltimore, Md.
Soriano House, Greenwich, Conn.
American Press Institute Conference Center, Reston, Va.
Atlanta Central Public Library, Atlanta, Ga.

1972 ▶ The MoMA, New York, dedicated its first exhibition on the life and work of a single, living architect to Marcel Breuer.
Saier House, Glanville, France
Neumann House, Pool House, Cronton-on-Hudson, N.Y.
Stillman House III, Litchfield, Conn.
Mundipharma Headquarters and Manufacturing Plant, Limburg, Germany
Grand Coulee Dam, Visitor Arrival Center, Grand Coulee, Wash.

1973
Southern New England Telephone Company, Traffic Service Position Systems Building, Torrington, Conn.
Gagarin House II, Litchfield, Conn.
Australian Embassy, Paris, France
Clarksburg Harrison Public Library, Clarksburg, W.Va.

1974
Convent of the Sisters of Divine Providence, Infirmary, Baldegg, Switzerland

1975
State University of New York, Faculty of Engineering and Applied Science Buildings Complex, Buffalo, N.Y.
Torrington Corporation, Penrith, Australia

1976 ▶ Breuer resigned from his practice for health reasons and moved to 63rd Street in Manhattan with his wife.

1981 ▶ Breuer died on July 1 in New York.

Europe

Germany:
Berlin
Interior Design for Piscator

Dessau
Jung Masters' Houses BAMBOS

Wiesbaden
Harnischmacher House

United Kingdom:
Bristol
Gane's Pavilion

France:
Glanville
Saier House

Flaine
Ski Resort

La Gaude
IBM Research Center

Paris
UNESCO Headquarters

Switzerland:
Moscia
Koerfer House

Zurich
Doldertal Houses

United States

Baltimore, Maryland
Hooper House II

Bismarck, North Dakota
Annunciation Priory of the Sisters of St. Benedict

Cleveland, Ohio
Cleveland Museum of Art

Collegeville, Minnesota
St. John's Abbey and University

Lakeville, Connecticut
Caesar Cottage

Lincoln, Massachusetts
Breuer House I

New Canaan, Connecticut
Breuer House II

Long Island, New York
Geller House I
Geller House II

New York, New York
MoMA Research House
University Heights Campus
Whitney Museum of American Art

Muskegon, Michigan
St. Francis de Sales Church

Wayland, Massachusetts
Chamberlain Cottage

Bibliography

Credits

▶ Argan, Guilio Carlo. *Marcel Breuer – disegno industriale e architettura*. Görlich editore, Milan, 1957.
▶ Blake, Peter. *Marcel Breuer. Architect and Designer*. The Museum of Modern Art, New York, 1949.
▶ Blake, Peter (ed.). *Marcel Breuer. Sun and Shadow. The Philosophy of an Architect*. Dodd, Mead & Co., New York, 1956.
▶ Driller, Joachim. *Marcel Breuer. Die Wohnhäuser 1923 – 1973*. Deutsche Verlags-Anstalt, Stuttgart, 1998.
▶ Droste, Magdalena and Manfred Ludewig. *Marcel Breuer. Design*. Taschen, Cologne, 1992.
▶ Gatje, Robert F. *Marcel Breuer. A Memoir*. Manocelli Press, New York, 2000.
▶ Hyman, Isabelle. *Marcel Breuer, Architect. The Career and the Buildings*. Harry N. Abrams, New York, 2001.
▶ Ichinowatari, Katsuhiko (ed.), "The Legacy of Marcel Breuer", in: *Process Architecture*, No. 32, Tokyo, 1982.
▶ Jones, Cranston. *Marcel Breuer 1921 – 1962*. Verlag Gerd Hatje, Stuttgart, 1962.
▶ Puente, Moisés and Lluís Ortega (eds.). "Marcel Breuer. Casas Americanas / American Houses", in: 2G. *Revista Internacional de Arquitectura* No. 17 (1) 2001, Barcelona, 2001.
▶ Papachristou, Tician. Marcel Breuer. New Buildings and Projects 1960 – 1970. Praeger Publishers, New York / Washington, 1970.
▶ Masello, David. Architecture Without Rules. *The Houses of Marcel Breuer and Herbert Beckhard*. W. W. Norton & Co., New York / London, 1993.
▶ Vegesack, Alexander von and Mathias Remmele (eds.). *Marcel Breuer. Design und Architektur*. Vitra Design Museum, Weil am Rhein, 2003.
▶ Wilk, Christopher. *Marcel Breuer. Furniture and Interiors*. Museum of Modern Art, New York, 1981.

The Author

Arnt Cobbers studied art history, history and music before writing a dissertation on medieval church architecture. After working as an architectural critic, he is now a freelance author in Berlin. Among his many publications are books on architecture in Berlin, as well as on the work of Frank Lloyd Wright, Mies van der Rohe, Karl Friedrich Schinkel, Ieoh Ming Pei and others. He is also the editor-in-chief of the music magazine *Partituren*.